How To Be A Positively Powerful Person!

About The Book

Overcoming childhood challenges, self defeating beliefs, a fear of writing, and total lack of business ownership skills, she was to become one of the country's first women to own and operate a national full service advertising agency. Today she is an author, public speaker, and president of Triad West, Inc. consulting and training. In her career, she has worked with leaders of major corporations, national nonprofit organizations, and federal and city officials. In appreciation of her expertise, others have invited her to come, speak, facilitate, and spread her message across the U.S., Puerto Rico, the Republic of South Africa, the United Kingdom, Latvia, Finland, Malaysia, and Russia.

Now, this dynamic woman tells her extraordinary success story and shares the user friendly tips that all dream makers use to create the impossible. This inspiring book will move you to be your most powerful best!

Joel Martin, Ph.D. believes that the key to breakthrough results in today's increasingly challenging world begin with *eight critical practices*. These practices are easy to understand and natural to follow once you know what they are. Part personal journey and part "help-yourself" guide, Joel's book is based on the strategies she's used with her corporate and entrepreneurial clients. She will show you how to *make your dreams come true* and succeed above and beyond ordinary expectations.

Whether you are just starting out, want to jump start a career, build a business, improve your personal relationships, advance your interpersonal communications, create breakthrough performance in a corporation, understand today's transformational technology, or just simply enjoy being better at everything that you do, this book will get you on the path you need to get there and show you how to be free and fearless while doing so!

Acclaim for *How To Be A Positively Powerful Person!*

"This is a wise, exceptional, and practical book. Dr. Joel Martin invites us to live positive powerful lives. She shows us with examples and models how to succeed in our relationships, business, family and community. Moving from beliefs to values, Dr. Martin constantly points us towards a fulfilled and committed life. I have found this book, like its author to be dynamic, revealing, empowering, and deeply caring. I recommend it to anyone who wants to know how to cultivate and sustain authentic power for one's self and others."
— **Bettie Spruill, CMEC, Transforming Begoro, Ghana Co-founder Ideal Coaching, Inc.**

"If you want something to be different, you have to think and do something different. *How To Be A Positively Powerful Person* got me going again! It is an instructional manual for people wanting to get out of a maze of procrastination."
— **John Atchison, John Atchison Salon and Products**

"The day I received the book I read it from cover to cover. It is inspirational and loaded with a lot of vital information we can use in our lives everyday. I highly recommend it as a must-read!!!!"
— **Dr. Edward Miller**

"These are the small lessons in life that make a BIG difference on the results that we have or don't have in our lives. In this book, Dr. Martin illustrates clearly how the power of our thinking, being, and doing impacts our latitude and our success with others. Thank you Dr. Martin for contributing and sharing yourself and your experiences with us."
— **Barbara Nunez, CSL, Principal of Cascades High School New York City Department of Education**

"Your book was very easy reading and the concepts that were laid out were very practical and easy to follow. Kudos to you!"

— **Linda G. Cooper, president, LGC & Associates Leadership for Global Competitiveness**

"Dr. Martin addresses a complicated and often misunderstood subject in a very straightforward manner. This insightful book is well written, easy to understand, and offers a concept that can make a difference in one's day-to-day life. Dr. Martin not only encourages the reader to strive to become a "positively powerful person" but also provides a step-by-step process to reach that goal."

— **Stan McLaughlin**
Former Vice President, Corporate Officer, Maritz Inc

"I would definitely recommend this book to others. I enjoyed so many aspects of the book. The style of writing is enjoyable to read, the authenticity of the author -- her warmth, sincerity and caring is apparent throughout, and heart-felt -- leaves the reader with wanting to know more about her. The content is inspiring and leaves the reader with the motivation to want to make changes in one's life immediately. There wasn't anything I didn't enjoy – please write another one!!!! Thank you so much for such a wonderful gift of yourself, for sharing the contribution of your expertise and for guiding me through the process of feeling like a truly Positive Powerful Woman. It feels so good to feel so alive and excited about what tomorrow will bring into my life."

— **Victoria Naylor**
Vice President Operations, Godfrey Children's Foundation

"Your book was easy to read and full of value for me personally and professionally. It challenged me to take a hard look at myself to see what else I can do to be a more powerful person. I recommend this book to everyone!"

—**Deborah J. Stokes, MSSA, LISW**
Social Work Administrator, Ohio Department of Health

"The book was very helpful in understanding the various aspects that make up a positive person, and also those things within you that make it difficult to be one. It is a "how to" book that simplifies an often misunderstood subject. I would highly recommend it for anyone who is looking for positive change in their lives."

— **Ley Borlo, Entrepreneur**

"This book resonates in my spirit and causes me to want to accomplish great things. As I flipped the pages, skimming at first, I was drawn in and taken hold of. I can see myself becoming a better person for my friends and family as a result. The exercises in the book gave me insights into things I had not considered in a long time. Dr. Joel Martin is one of the most powerful and professional trainers I have ever worked with. She has an intuitive sense of the core "goings on" with people. I have been amazed at how she can see inside a person's heart and bring out their true spirit. In working with Joel, I would trust her to coach my mom, dad, brother, or sister; she is that good! I recommend her new book *How To Be A Positively Powerful Person!* to anyone who is looking for an edge in being successful in life."

— **Lorne Epstein**
Author, President of E3

"Dr. Martin, a dedicated and extremely perceptive visionary within the truest meaning and application of the concept, possesses many positive attributes heightened by warm and particularly strong interpersonal skills. She is a highly effective communicator; extremely creative; recognizes and subscribes to the concept of respect for the dignity and worth of individuals; tenacious in follow-through of programmatic thrusts for which she has leadership responsibility; and, equally as effective in support of those programs and projects led by others viewed as being beneficial."

— **Chuck Smith, Principal**
The Chuck Smith Organization

We chose Joel Martin's firm because of their reputation as one of the best in the nation for delivering breakthrough leadership performance and organization change…You have set us straight on how great we are and how great we can become. You don't let us get away with anything less than our best. Each one of us who has made a decision with you, who has been in a meeting facilitated by you, or who has been trained by you comes away a better person both professionally and personally.

— **Leslie Warren,**
Vice President, ABHOW

How To Be A Positively Powerful Person!

How To Be
A Positively Powerful Person!

The Steps, The Practices & The Tools To Access Your Positive Power

Joel Martin, Ph.D.

SUGAR PUP PRODUCTIONS

HOW TO BE A POSITIVELY POWERFUL PERSON. Copyright © 2003 by Joel Martin, PhD. All rights reserved. Printed in the United States of America. No part of this book may be used or reproduced or transmitted in any form or by any means, electronic or mechanical, including photocopying, recording, or by any information storage and retrieval system without written permission from the publisher except in the case of brief quotations embodied in critical articles and reviews. For information address Sugar Pup Productions, 9616 East Southwind Lane, Scottsdale, AZ 85262-3658. Fax (480) 563-5586.

SUGAR PUP books, tapes, and other products may be purchased for educational, business, or sales promotional use. For information please write: Sugar Pup Productions, 9616 East Southwind Lane, Scottsdale, AZ 85262-3658. Fax (480) 563-5586.

First paperback edition printed 2003.
Second paperback edition printed 2004

The Library of Congress has cataloged the first edition as follows: How to be a positively powerful person / by Joel Martin, PhD. – 1st edition.

Copyright Registration: TX 5-856-431
ISBN 0-9752970-051995

Cover Art: Bob Martin
Cover and Content Design: Joel Martin
Editor: Elizabeth Zack
Clipart: Office/Microsoft.com

SUGAR PUP PRODUCTIONS

*Dedicated to Mom and Dad, Cybel and Bob.
Without you, this would not have
been possible.*

Contents

Foreword XIII
Acknowledgements XVII
Introduction: My Story XXIII

1. The Power of Beliefs 1
2. The Power of Feedback 21
3. The Power of Education 29
4. The Power of Make-Believe 37
5. The Power of Choice 49
6. The Power of Responsibility & Accountability 67
7. The Power of Values 81
8. The Power of Purpose 109
9. The Power of Vision Creation 113
10. The Power of Dedication 135

About The Author 139

Foreword

The title of this book hits the nail on the head in terms of an important goal we should all seek in life. Through my life's work I have found that it takes positive relationships to nurture the true powerful person within. I firmly believe that through networking, the building of relationships and the mutual leveraging of these resources, we can gain a positive outlook on life, and the power to fulfill its worth. I have had the pleasure of building an effective and productive relationship with Dr. Joel Martin, one born out of networking, which for me is the true meaning of success. I am a proponent of networking because I know its merits. So let me say this:

Networking works when you fully understand that there is *inherent value* in every human being and every human relationship regardless of title or position. Only when we mature enough to stop *prejudging* people as to their worthiness of our assistance can we truly give without expectation. When you give first, without expectation, you are networking for the benefit of others, and therefore the law of increasing returns will reward you tenfold. There are no expectations to this law. Had the people in my life prejudged me because I lived in publicly subsidized tenement housing or because I mopped floors at La Guardia Airport, I would never have had the assistance I needed to fully blossom and maximize my full human potential. This probably would be the case with most Black people. This is the spiritual and philosophical underpinning of effective networking.

Networking works when you understand that there is very little that you can do or have in life without working with other people. Therefore, you work diligently on building and developing your infrastructure of human resources.

Networking works when you understand that the whole is greater than the sum of its parts. Networks must be built upon a foundation of established relationships, first of all, but they can extend beyond. Building that essential foundation, however, takes time. To create one, you must have an established rapport with your key core of networking contacts.

Networking works when you can comfortably and successfully match needs and resources. Creating a win-win situation is the optimum, and although it may not always be exactly an even exchange, often things work out that way in the long run.

If, at first glance, you do not appear to have an established network base of close friends and contacts, you need not despair. You probably do have the necessary foundation, but you simply have not yet recognized your friends and other associates as the base of your network. As adults, on average we each know at least five hundred to seven hundred people on a casual or social basis. If you multiply that number of contacts by the number of people each of them knows, then your extended network of secondary contacts—friends of friends, colleagues of colleagues—is mind-boggling!

There have been many studies to document the power of the extended network, but one of the most renowned is that of sociologist Mark Granovetter. Entitled "The Strength of Weak Ties," it was presented in the *American Journal of Sociology*. Granovetter found that acquaintances are more likely than family or friends to give individuals direct information and to recommend opportunities to them. These acquaintances, he found, are often only two or three contacts away. With the right interpersonal skills, you can be successful in attracting their assistance, even though you do not have personal relationships with them.

Perhaps most important to making networking work is showing appreciation for the contributions of your fellow networkers. Remember how your mother labored to instill gratitude in you? ("Now, say 'thank you!'") Well, as usual, your mother knew best. Expressing gratitude is positive reinforcement. *It works.* I make a point to thank people just for making a call for me or sending me some special article they think I might be interested in. All of this takes time, but it is time invested toward a larger reward...that of being a positively powerful person. Thank you, Dr. Martin, for this insightfully written book.

– George C. Fraser, Author
Success Runs In Our Race: The Complete Guide to Effective Networking in the Black Community

Acknowledgments

I am writing this book in appreciation of my family: the Kenneys, McLaurins, Martins, Carters, Pembertons, my godmother Aunt Ida Burks, my sisters and brothers (Annette, Carolyn, Kim, Kelly, Curtis, Keith, Karl Jr., and adopted sis Nakia), the "Greenies": Barbara Selvey, Francis Ben, Loraine Smith, Sylvia Sears, Shanna Mayes, and Debbie Stokes. The other best friends I grew up with Judy Gray Wright and Marie Reddick. Also Frankie, who opened the door, and Fred Prendergast who introduced me to Annette Prendergast.

The transformationalists: Nelson Frye, Bettie Spruill, George Fraser, Joyce Christie, Dr. Ray Blanchard, Dr. Adrienne Anderson, Dr. Belinda Hartnett, Duane Smotherman, Glen Lechtanski, Raquel Rodriguez, Veronica Conway, Travis Anderson, Stuart Gelles, Jib Ellison, Van Carney, Joe Rosenberg, Christopher Parker, Sylvia Wilkins-High, Debi Lewinson, Jon Furner, Lorne Epstein, Barbara Nunez, Barbara Lindsey, Bessie House Soremekun, Carole Copeland Thomas, Cheryl Broussard, Darrell Miller Esq., Dennis Kimbro, Les Brown, Frances Wright, Gasby Greely Brown, George Christopher Scott, Gerry Foster, Hosiah Huggins Jr., Hattie Hill, Jesse

Brown, Jewel Diamond Taylor, JoAnn Holly, Kym Yancey, Linda Coleman-Willis, Marilyn French Hubbard Ph. D, Melvin Gravely, Michele Adams Proctor, Paul Bryant, Ralph Thomas, Reggie Williams, Stacia Robinson, Stedman Graham, Sherry Winston, and Yvette Moyo. Camille Odeh, Scott Aaseng, Linda James, Jazz Fenton, Clinton Terrell, Jack Swizick, Terry Nelson, Jim Earl, Ellen Ivy Le Coff, Traci Reandeau, Warren Cole, Marlene Fain, Steven Reed, Beverly Bernard, Joanne Brady, Melissa Zeligman, Kevin Coutinho, the Hanley Family, Dr. Julie Smith, Dr. Leslie Wilkes-Braksick, and again, my husband Bob.

The entrepreneurial and corporate visionary clients, artists, co-workers, and educators I've worked with, contributed to, and learned from: Charles Richardson the originator of the Triad name, David Ferguson, Leslie Warren, Earl Graves, Ed Lewis, Clarence Smith, Susan L. Taylor, Waymon Smith, Henry Brown, Victor Julien, Byron Lewis, Carolyn Jones, Tom Burrell, Ken Smikle, Reginald Lyles, Geri Luongo, Gale Hollingsworth, George Edwards, Sydney Small, Percy Sutton Sr., John Atchison, Dr. Joseph Duffy, Terrie Williams, Jeffrie Story, Wallace Graham, Sheila Burke, Stephanie Barnette, John Procope, Carolyn Odum, Lonnell "Lonnie" Brewer, Lorrinda Gray-Davis, Garry Walters, Angela and George Brooks, David Milliner, Rodd Rodriguez, dear friend Denise Edwards Young, Arn Ashwood, Byron Jones, Sakeena Gittens Shaw, Pat Stevenson, Dana Suggs, Carolyn Henson, and Robin Miles. Professor Art Warmoth, Neil Neveras, and my Wharton Fellows Three colleagues, particularly J. Allen

Kosowsky, Brenda Shore, Yong Kwek Ping, and Chris Liedel. My friend and co-creative partner Susan Sydney McCall and also from my early ad agency days, Fred Peterman, George Newell, Bonny Newell, JoAnne Curley, and Tom Yohe, what a great group to work with at McCaffrey McCall. For their spiritual guidance: My ministers Rev. Katherine Ward and Rev. Benjamin N. Thomas, Sr.

The board and organization members I've served with especially the National Alliance of Market Developers: H. Naylor Fitzhugh, LeBaron Taylor, Chuck Morrison, Bill Toles, Marquetta Glass, Earl Harvey, Deborah Crable, Robert Acquaye, Derrick Brockman, Gladys Hoffler-Thomas, Frank Clay, Hiram Smith, Derrick Brockman, Susan J. Eddington, Danette Render, Opal Freeman, Michael House, Wendell Niles, Julia Holmes MAS, Deborah Crable, Gale Harris, Tierney DeCuir, Jonathan Metcalf, Norm Bond, Christopher Mack, Wendell Niles, Donna Beasley, Linda Brown Ph.D, Karen Austin, Camille Erkins, James Freese, William Bernard Smoots, James "Bud" Ward, Clyde C. Allen, and Willetta Willis-McGhee. The American Red Cross: Cathy Tisdale, Pedro Ayala, Ruth Parris, and especially the Grand Canyon Chapter. The Grand Canyon Black Chamber of Commerce: Cody Williams and Marquis Scott. Dr. Rev. Ann Williamson, Choo Tay, Jennifer Swan, Kendall Cooper, Kevin Fletcher, Linda Cooper, Manuel V. Cisneros, Marc Cobb, Steven Connor, Victoria Naylor, and Olivia Simmons.

Many professionals assisted me. I would like to thank my editor Elizabeth Zack of BookCrafters LLC (www.bookcraftersllc.com), for the professional guidance and editing she provided; Bob Martin, for the beautiful artwork for the cover (www.triadwest.com/themartingallery.html); George Fraser for his foreword and guidance; Ramon Williamson for his coaching; and Express Media (www.expressmedia.com) for their printing services.

Many other positively powerful people also influenced me. If I haven't mentioned your name I apologize for the oversight. I truly have been blessed with brilliant colleagues as well as loving friends and family.

And, last but not least, I am also writing this book for me.

How To Be
A Positively Powerful Person!

Introduction

My Story

She was raised by her mother to tell the truth, respect her elders, and believe that she could be anything that she wanted to be, "even the president of the United States." When she was eight years old, her schoolteacher gave the class a homework assignment of writing a poem. That night as she wrote her poem, the words flew. The child assumed that this ability to create pictures out of words came from her mother, because her mother inspired her in all ways.

Her mother, a very loving and loved woman, wrote poems and decorated them with little pictures. She was also a voracious reader, and had passed this love on to the child. So after the eight year old finished her poem she felt "wow..." and was very proud.

The next day she took her poem to her school, and when called upon, she stood in front of her classmates to read it. She beamed during the reading. However, her pride and joy were drowned by the harsh, angry tones of the teacher, who demanded to know, "Who wrote that? I know *you* didn't!"

The eight-year-old was humiliated, embarrassed, confused, and shocked into numbness. *The teacher must be speaking the truth as she's an adult,* she thought. Plus her mother had taught her to trust authority figures. She was caught in a double bind.

This feeling of humiliation remained with the little girl long after the actual incident. What she remembered was that she had been ordained by her teacher to be an "eight-year-old who was not only dumb but a liar who was incapable of writing poetry."

This is a true story. Likely you've guessed that it happened to me. This event was the basis for many of my life choices and challenges. It is no wonder that I chose to major in fine arts instead of liberal arts in college, that I chose to be an art director at an ad agency, and that escaping into fictional books was easier for me than studying academic nonfiction. Writing became tortuous for me and as for speaking in front of groups--forget it!

Completing this book has been a battle. That's one of the reasons, though, that I wrote it. I wrote it to prove something to myself and to be a gift to others.

When I was about three there was a more senior event in my life. My birth father deserted my mother and me. I remember always feeling sad as a child because I didn't have a father. I also felt sorry for my mother, as she was now alone. This event was another bit of the foundation for the ideas I was to have growing up. Even though I had close cousins, nurturing aunts and uncles, and a great godmother, it was tough to grow up without a father.

From this I decided that men were not to be trusted, that for me to be vulnerable and create any kind of a long-term relationship with anyone was impossible, and that I didn't want one anyway if the result was to be what happened to my mother. I was afraid to commit. People wouldn't love me, and "they" would leave just like my father did, so why bother.

I have told many people by now how these two events shaped my life, and I've found that they are not isolated occurrences. This, and worse, has happened to others. However, I could not find any solace in the company of others whom I did not truly know.

Was it true that I was dumb, a liar, and incapable of being loved and having a committed relationship? *No.* But that's how I acted. Fortunately, my mother also taught me that if I worked hard enough I could accomplish *anything...* eventually.

My path to knowing and coaching others on how to be positively powerful began long ago with a training course. By then I was married. My husband Bob and I had our daughter Cybel. But these and all other relationships were not what they could be for the reasons given above. My husband and I were introduced to the training program by our friend, Denise Edwards. This program changed my life. Through it I found my passion and a calling to be in service to others. I realized I wanted to coach others on how to bring their dreams to life. This is what makes me happy.

Through the program I discovered that responsibility and burden weren't the same, that leadership is about making a difference, that life is precious and not to be squandered, that a vision is something that is not (that doesn't exist) but could be with my commitment, and more. I thrived on the intensity of the group encounters and found them to be the peak transformational experiences of my life. It was through this training program that I began to see the potential of a whole new way of life for myself.

To give you an idea of what it felt like to me: Imagine that you are walking along a path in a dense forest. The path dips down through valleys and up steep hills until it finally leads you to a clearing where the grass is a carpet of brilliant green. You sit and experience a sense of peace, and you breathe a sigh of relief because you've made it through the forest.

Eventually, you look around and notice that there's a barely discernible continuation of the path on  the other side of the glen. Trees with spikes and vines share pinpoints of light, and strange sounds seem to emanate from there. You experience trepidation and uncertainty about leaving this tranquil spot you've found, and consider whether you should return the way you came. But eventually you stand and proceed to the path ahead. With persistence, you attack the undergrowth, the spikes, and your fear.

BAM! You stumble forward and to your amazement, you realize that you have come to another clearing where there's a party being given in your honor, with your friends, family, and coworkers. There's also a sign on a magnificent and beautiful house that says, "Welcome home. All this is yours."

In the language of dreams, the house was me, and I was a giving, powerful, joyous, loving, playful, and open woman! One who was much more than the sum total of her childhood experiences.

What I discovered was that losing my birthfather early in life and being called a liar weren't the worst things that could have happened to me. *Instead, they were two of the greatest gifts that a powerfully positive woman with a passion for people could have been given.* I wouldn't be who I am today without those events.

I want you to know that my life was pretty good before I took the training courses. I had accomplished a lot in my life, career-wise. I was the president and creative director of New York City-based JP Martin Associates, Inc., a full-service ad agency Bob and I co-founded. My company was the agency of record for the world's largest beer company, and we developed and introduced a new malt beverage with them. We assisted one of the leading hair care companies with a new product launch. We had award-winning art and copy people, an original music production team, and producers, all of whom worked together wonderfully. I was considered one of the leaders in our niche of the industry. I was featured on the cover of *Essence,* and in *Fortune* and *Newsweek,* and had been on the Today Show. On a personal level, Cybel, Bob and I were together, and we had a close, loving family, although at that time we were nowhere as close as we are now.

After I completed the training curriculum, the question that I kept asking myself, no matter how much I attempted to ignore it, was, *"What do I want to do with the rest of my life? Make a difference with a human being, or sell another bottle of beer?"* Even though I struggled with accepting the answer, the answer was an "of course."

My heart was no longer in the agency business. As a result I hired staff to do what I no longer was interested in doing. (Today I would sell the company but at the time I didn't know that was possible.) When our largest account fired us, I resigned other accounts and closed the 15 year-old agency Bob and I founded.

Even though I knew advertising wasn't my passion any longer closing my company was traumatic and humbling. We auctioned off nearly all of our furniture and JP Martin Associates, Inc. was no more. But Dr. Joel Martin was on her way to becoming, and Robert S. Martin, the agency co-owner, was on his way to being a full-time oil painter. I asked Bob later what he thought would have happened to him if we had kept the agency going. He said, *"I'd probably be dead."*

I am glad that we paid the price then to live the life we wanted, rather than to live a life of regrets. As I would later be advising others, we pay our prices now, or later, with penalties and interest.

After Cybel graduated from high school and moved to Philadelphia where she would attend college, Bob and I moved to Northern California. Within three years I had become a workshop facilitator and second level trainer in the most intense of the training company's programs. Within another three years, I was a corporate trainer with corporate training guru Nelson Frye and his company. Within another two, I had opened my own training company and was a training designer and facilitator of change through team building, leadership development, human potential effectiveness, diversity, corporate alignment, and other trainings.

After I got over myself and into others, I got curious about why experiential training is so powerful and what were its origins. These questions put me on another path through the unknown. I earned a Masters in Psychology, a doctorate in Communications, and a Wharton Fellowship. I have put to rest "the dumb little eight-year-old liar" conversation in me. And Bob and I are celebrating more than 30 years of our deeply committed relationship and marriage. Thankfully, with regards to my being loving and being loved, "I can't" has become an overwhelmingly "*Yes, I can!*"

I loved my training. It was a catalyst for my change. Now, as a consultant, speaker, and trainer, I know intimately how training can shorten the gap between what is and what we want it to be--whatever the "it" is. When speed matters, training assists us in creating the desired skills, attitudes, and knowledge we need to move to the next level of success. Training is capable of providing a way for us to develop a common language, goals, and tactics for accomplishing greatness together.

I decided to write this book to share what I've learned and taught in trainings and through speeches. After one particularly powerful 'conversation' with 2,000 women in Columbus, Ohio I was kicking myself that I didn't have a book to leave with them so that they could continue the great work that we had begun together. The conversation was "L.E.A.D. to Success" and it was about the power of leadership, entrepreneurship, and diversity. I decided then and there that I would conquer my fear of writing a book and get busy.

So for them and future audiences, I made a commitment to share some of knowledge I have available about *enhancing personal power*. I will give you the steps, the coaching, and the questions that you can use to turn on your personal power source so brightly that others may be blinded by your brilliance.

Inside, you'll find the thinking behind transformational training processes, quotes, poetry, business examples, and personal stories to make this book very user-friendly for you. There will be exercises designed just for you, so that you can explore the principles in terms of your own life. Answer the questions I offer you *sequentially* to get the maximum value out of them.

I believe that everyone has the ability to be a positively powerful person, to tap into their beliefs, core values, personal purpose, guiding vision, and poignant stories in such a way that they are able to consistently empower themselves and others, and that they can repeatedly create their dreams. *It may not be easy, but it is possible.*

In Chapter One, we take on our beliefs and how they can enhance or sabotage our power. We also discuss what to do when we catch ourselves running into negativity in our minds.

In Chapter Two, we'll explore one of the most precious gifts we can receive and get from another. (And it's perfectly *free*!) We'll delve also into the *all-star method* for checking others' beliefs about us, which we do through obtaining — and accepting! — Feedback.

In Chapter Three, we decide on the gift you will give yourself. You will plot your learning goals as well.

In Chapter Four, we will go to the land where anything is possible, a place where true creativity and vision begins. We will pay our respects to our imaginations in the land of make-believe. As children we knew the power of our imaginations. *As adults, we all can still use this ability to direct our futures.*

In Chapter Five, we'll go through a simulation that will tap into the power of choice we each possess and that can never be taken away.

In Chapter Six, we'll connect our freedom to choose with the concepts of personal responsibility and accountability. We'll explore the differences between living life as a victim and being victimized. So get ready.

In Chapter Seven, we'll explore the mighty power of values. You will figure out which values are critical to you, and how to live your life according to them.

In Chapter Eight, we'll bring all of the forces together and identify the steps needed for making your vision, the compelling future that matters to you real, which is what positively powerful people do.

In the Chapter Nine, the next to the last chapter, we'll take the path that all dream makers take to create the impossible.

In Chapter Ten, we'll put all of the power forces together that you need to climb to the top of your mountain and celebrate the power of dedication.

May you find what I share in this book of value, support, and inspiration, for it comes from my heart to yours. I believe everyone deserves access to the principles that lead to becoming a positively powerful person.

Imagine how the world would be if everyone lived their dreams…beginning with *you*. And if you had the power to make a dream come true, what would it be?

Let's begin.

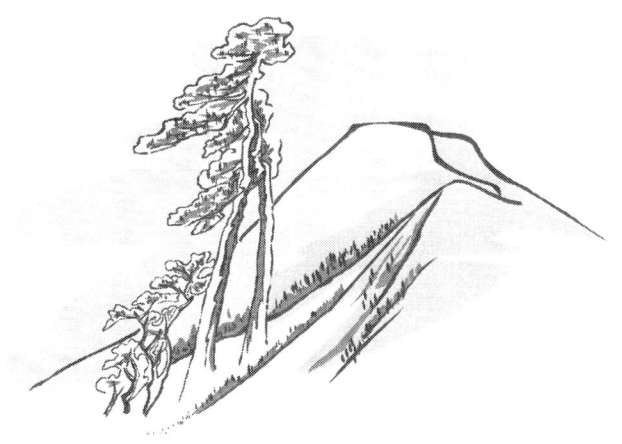

Chapter One

The Power of Beliefs: The Start of It All

You can control what you think: Free will is God's greatest gift to us. Our thinking is the basis of all our difficulties – it's at the heart of our insecurities and of problems in our relationships, the root cause of every conflict in the world. If we want a new and better life, our thinking has to be new and better.

Susan L. Taylor
Editorial Director, *Essence* Magazine

When I held my new baby daughter in my arms for the first time, she was from that moment on adorable, precious, and perfect. She looked just like my husband Bob, with a little bit of me mixed in.

I could go on describing the beauty and virtues of our child, but let me ask you to think about your baby, a family member's baby, or any child about one year old. *What do you notice about them?* I have asked that question many times in my workshops, and I always get the same answers: Vulnerable, loving, curious, innocent, tender, giving, demanding, caring, enthusiastic, open, and happy. Well, those qualities are true most of the time, and when they are not, it's because the children are either hungry or wet.

As a baby grows older, things happen, and a child begins to make cause and effect connections between the actions of the people in his or her life, like Mom, Dad, brothers, sisters, and others. "If she does this… then this happens" is the equation that fires up his or her brain. And through thought, word, deed, facial expression, tone of voice, body language, physical touch, or lack of physical touch, the child comes into contact with feelings of pleasure or pain.

A little one learns early on that if he or she throws a tantrum, he or she will get picked up, hit, or ignored. If she or he wants a hug and love, this action will result in this response from Mom or Dad. That if Mommy says, "you're a good little girl" or "you're a bad little girl" it must be so.

We each come into the world as perfectly positive powerful little people, but as a result of what we decide about the actions, words or lack of action and words of others, we little boys and girls will either grow up feeling loved or unloved, wanted or unwanted, precious or unimportant. By the age of five our core set of beliefs about ourselves and the world around us are formed.

Over time, we decide the beliefs that will shape our lives. For example, complete these sentences with the *first thought* that comes into your mind:

Women are _____

Men are _____

Work is _____

I am _____

Life is _____

Family is _____

Whatever words you used to fill in the blank *is a belief based on your past experiences.*

It is important for you to become aware of your beliefs in order to accomplish your goals. You must come to know the beliefs that work for you and those that don't; you need to know your power sources and your power drains. As a trainer buddy of mine says, "Your beliefs define your horizon of possibilities."

If I keep on saying to myself that I cannot do a certain thing, it is possible that I may end by really becoming incapable of doing it. On the contrary, if I have the belief that I can do it, I shall surely acquire the capacity to do it even if I may not have it at the beginning.

Mahatma Gandhi

Your beliefs also determine what is right and what is wrong for you. Rightness is what is consistent with your belief system. Our minds can justify anything to be right. People can break up relationships to be right. They can dead wrong driving on the highway wanting to be right.

The diagram on the next page shows how our beliefs shape our lives. Use it as a resource to understand yourself and others better.

How Your Beliefs Shape Your Success

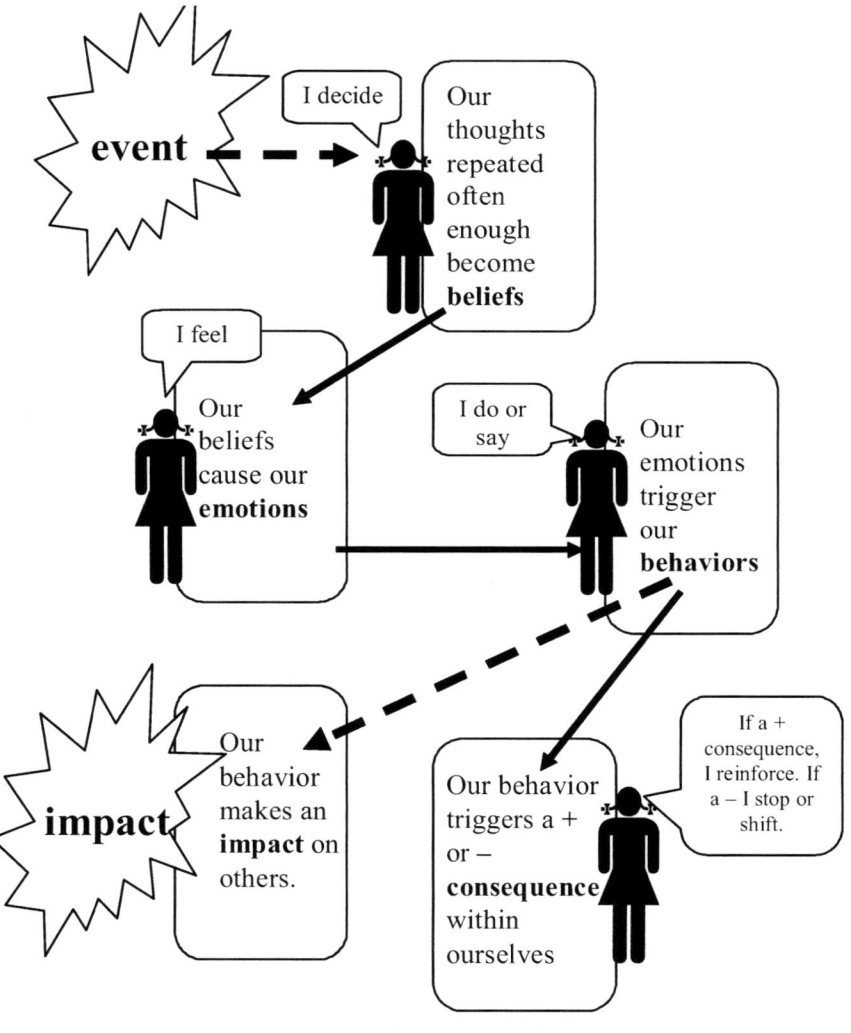

There is an expression, "If I see it, I'll believe it." I believe it is more accurate to say, *"If I believe it, I'll see it."*

Imagine someone saying something derogatory about one of your closest friends. No matter how much they may try to get you to see this friend through their eyes, they can't because *you don't believe what they are saying is true.* Our beliefs are *fixed* until we challenge them, take them on, resolve them, handle them, and change them. No one can make us change them; *we have to be willing to do this on our own.* And this is what positively powerful people do — all the time.

If you want to unleash the power you possess to change your beliefs, there is a way to begin:

- You must first *want* to become aware of your beliefs: what you consider the good, the bad, and the ugly. This takes facing up to your 'stuff.' Your stuff is like baggage that you don't want to carry any longer such as feeling like a victim, having low self esteem, etc.

- Once you're aware of your beliefs, you then need to ask yourself, "Does this belief work for me or not?" Here are questions to ask yourself to determine whether a belief works for you: Does it lead to my feeling more powerful or less powerful? Does it empower me to be actively engaged in accomplishments or does it take me off my path to success? Does it serve my highest self?

- If it does work, keep the belief. If the belief doesn't work for you, recognize that it's time to handle it and replace it.

- If it doesn't work for you, do your best to find the source, the beginning point where you think you first started believing that way. If you have difficulty figuring out the source, look to the two examples of my non-working beliefs about myself in the Introduction of this book. *Your beliefs too may have arisen because of some experience you had in childhood, so try to THINK BACK!*

- Once you've come up with a source, ask yourself, "What value is there in my giving this event my power?" The events in the past are history – or herstory. They are over and done with. It may be time to let these remembrances go, to release them, to forgive yourself or another. Awareness of the source is a step forward for the positively powerful.

- Now, about the belief. Ask yourself, "If I keep believing this way, what do I get out of it?" This will show you the payoffs you receive. In my story the payoffs I got were that I didn't need to try to write or trust others. I got to be right about the way my life was and why I had the results that I had. Being right meant I didn't need to risk. My payoff was that I got to stay in my comfort zone.

- Next ask, "If I keep believing this way, what are the *prices* I will pay?" The prices I paid were that I may have missed out on new relationships and educational accomplishments.

- Now it's time to ask yourself a critical question, "Is my belief true or is it false?" A belief is simply *something we hold to be true and act as if it is.* As I explained earlier, it's what we started to believe as children. But what if it *ain't* so?! Beliefs are *not* facts like the fact that gravity is a force on earth. Beliefs are things that we've decided and to which we make automatic connections. For example, I could have decided that my third-grade teacher was having a bad day and was being cranky or that she wished she could write a beautiful poem as I did; who knows what the truth of that day actually was?

- It's important to add that you may get to the source, know the belief is not true, be aware of your prices, and your pay offs and still *not feel any better.* MOVE ON ANYWAY! Put a smile on your face, get out of your comfort zone, and get on with it.

A colleague asked me, what if the belief works for you but doesn't work for someone else? That is a great question, and here is what I told her: If it works for you and not for someone else, you have a conflict and a choice to make. You can notice the disagreement and continue on your course. Or you can let the other person know your intention and do what it takes to understand the way they believe. And continue on your course. It is likely the latter strategy will be a relationship builder and that you will learn something in the process.

There are positively powerful beliefs that move you forward. But there are also dream-slaying limiting beliefs. You must take on the beliefs that seem most important if you want to be successful and feel fulfilled. It's up to you to decide whether a belief is positive or negative, empowering or sabotaging, ridiculous or understandable. And you do this based on whether it works for you, and whether it gets you where you want to go. Again, if it doesn't work for you, if it sabotages what you say you want, *get rid of it and replace it with another*.

As my colleague Duane Smotherman says, "Beliefs are like clothes in a closet…some fit, some don't." When you do spring-cleaning in your "beliefs closet" you can sort through the beliefs that work, that don't work, and that you need to send to goodwill because you've outgrown them. If I'd been committed to being right about my childhood belief about men, I'd have stayed married for one year and then quit, so that I could make sure that I was the one to leave first. Fortunately I realized that something needed to go — and it was my belief, and not me or my husband! Yes, beliefs define what we say is right and wrong, and what we think will come true. They form the boundaries of our comfort zones. If you are willing to challenge your beliefs, what is possible?

Your Beliefs Define Your Mental Comfort Zone

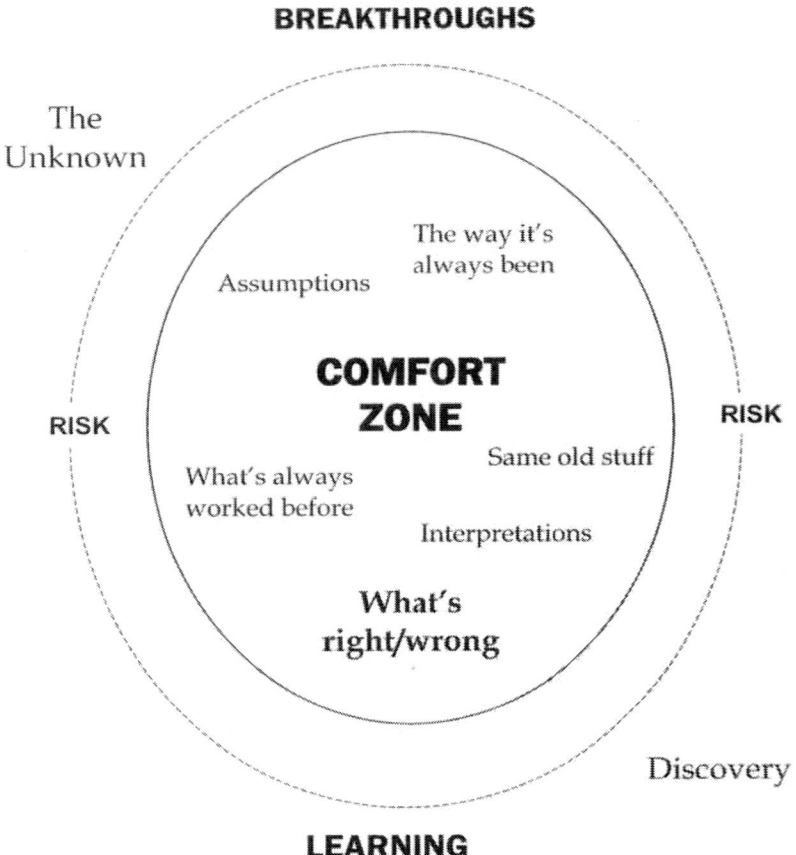

Only those going too far will know how far they can go.

Remember what it feels like to do spring-cleaning? For me there is a feeling of happiness as I begin; then a feeling of accomplishment as I look back at the cleaned up space. *Notice the feelings you have as a result of your commitment to being aware, and the sorting through and clearing out activities you engage in as a result. Do you feel empowered as a result? Inspired? Positive?* Chances are you do, and that you don't feel down. You'll probably even discover that as a result of your new mindset your goals seem closer and easier to reach.

So it's time now to clear out your "beliefs closet." As you notice the emotions that come up for you in this process, write about them. This is an important part of the clearing out process too, because beliefs trigger emotions.

My suggestion is to start with the beliefs that deal with the most important people in your life. Here are some ideas to get you started:

- My beliefs about my mother are…

- My beliefs about my father are…

- My beliefs about my sister/brother(s) are…

- My beliefs about myself are…

But you're not done yet. There are a many other beliefs that impact you and your life. So continue on figuring out your beliefs about…

- My beliefs about my self-image are… *Do you see yourself as confident, sexy, shy, etc.*

- My beliefs about my spirituality are… *Are you a spiritual person? Religious? Is spirituality even important to you?*

- My beliefs about my love life, sex life, and intimate relationships are…

- My beliefs about my career are…

- My beliefs about my finances are…

- My beliefs about my intelligence and education are…

- My beliefs about my home are…

- My beliefs about my body are… *Is it your temple? Or are you embarrassed about it?*

- My beliefs about my health are… *Is it related to the life expectancy of relatives?*

The important thing to remember is: *if you want to become powerful, challenge your nonproductive beliefs.*

Freedom is not a vacation from earthly responsibilities and eternal realities; it is actually quite the opposite.
In freedom, we finally get to do everything ourselves.
We get to see a need and meet it because it's the right thing to do....Freedom is hard work.

Dr. Myles Monroe
Founder and President of Bahamas Faith Ministries, Speaker, and Author

---

There are millions of events in your life, from the moment you wake up to the time that you fall asleep, and in between. Life is a series of them. And, how you approach these events with your beliefs determines your ability to experience personal power. Whether you feel sad, depressed, numb, happy, hate, fear, anger, elation, joy, excitement, fondness, love, or lust is connected to your *belief* about the event.

The phone rings. Someone taps you on the shoulder. You watch an exciting movie. You walk into a bakery where they are taking fresh cinnamon rolls out of the oven. The man you've fallen for walks by your desk after he's stood you up for the fifth time. You remember the last time you met with your mother. *Whatever the event, one or more of your senses gets triggered.* Your hearing, smelling, seeing, touching, and/or tasting sense(s) go into action. It's no surprise that when we're sad (thinking sad thoughts) we are more apt to get sick.

Your beliefs shape your attitudes. Your attitudes shape your results. "You can't get the latitude if you don't have the attitude." *So if you want to change your situation you need to change your attitude.* Neuro-Linguistic Programming and other theories of change say that changing attitudes (the domain of beliefs) is more effective than changing skills (capabilities), behavior, or environment (external surroundings).

In our comfort zones are all of our beliefs, habits, current knowledge, skills, and attitudes. In our comfort zones, we do things automatically, based upon what we're used to. If we habitually stay in this zone, we will always have, maintain, and generate the S.O.S., the same old stuff. So take it a step further: if we keep doing what we have always done based on what we have always believed, what we will always get? What we already have. We will maintain the status quo.

Is this bad or wrong? No. But ask yourself, *is staying in your comfort zone allowing you to live up to your highest aspirations?* I suggest not. Is it limiting your contribution to others and yourself in terms of the relationship you could have with them? Yes. Does it allow you to handle the stress, threat of violence, and chaos of today's world? No! *Only outside of your comfort zone can you create the impossible thing you envision – your dream.* Stick with me, and you'll discover that positively powerful people are uncomfortable being *too* comfortable!

Our beliefs trigger feelings, and feelings trigger behaviors. If we are taught, "children should be seen and not heard" when having an opportunity to speak in front of a group, how will we feel? Nervous and anxious. How will we act? Shy and withdrawn.

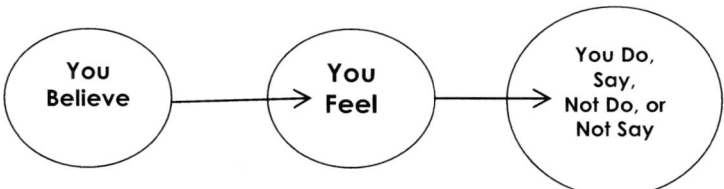

If we believe a business environment is an inappropriate setting for emotions, how do we feel when we need to show our vulnerability and passion about a project? Stressed and closed off. How will we act? With restraint, quiet, and without allowing ourselves to express excitement.

If we are told anything often enough as children, we believe it. Tennis ace Serena Williams remembers her father telling her at age 6, "You're going to be a tennis champion." She says now, "I just grew up believing it."

What are the examples you've chosen from your life? Take a look. Notice the connection between the belief, the feeling, and your behaviors. Then ask yourself what other possibilities are there that could lead to your success.

Payoffs

As human beings we don't do anything without a reason. We want the payoff that occurs as a result of our actions, the WIIFM (what's in it for me). We've all used the word "consequences," but generally that word has a negative spin, not a positive one. In behavioral science theory and practice it has a neutral spin.

Technically defined, behavioral consequences are those things and events that follow a behavior and change the probability that the behavior will be repeated in the future.

Dr. Aubrey C. Daniels
President, Precision Learning Systems and Author

Powerfully positive people are aware of the impact they have on others. From my studies of behavioral science, I've learned the four ways of communicating that influence behavior. By identifying them and using them intentionally in your life, you will produce effects. While I will use a joke to explain each communication type, keep in mind that the dynamic holds true for *any* situation.

Positive Reinforcement

If you use positive reinforcement with others then you *increase the likelihood* that they will continue acting in the way you've reinforced. For example, James tells you a joke. You find it hilarious and laugh at the punch line. Then you give him a warm friendly smile and say, "That was pretty funny." James feels he's brightened your day and made you happy. You can bet you will be hearing more of James's jokes.

Negative Reinforcement

Here's how negative reinforcement works. Mike at the office tells you a joke that is inappropriate. Maybe it has a sexist or racist spin to it. You don't want to hear anymore of this kind of joke and want to *escape or avoid* this kind of joke in the future. So you give Mike a reprimand, a stern look, and tell him you will report him if he continues telling jokes like that. It's safe to say Mike will not be telling you any more jokes.

Punishment

Barbara tells you a joke in private, and you think it's the funniest thing you've ever heard. So at the office staff meeting, you tell everybody about her joke. Rather than telling the actual joke, though, you say, "Barbara, tell everybody the joke you told me" and look expectedly her way. Now, Barbara is a shy person. She is uncomfortable and doesn't want to tell the joke. She ends up wishing she'd never told you the joke in the first place. In this kind of punishment, your intention may have been positive but you have *negatively penalized* her by your action. Barbara's jokes will stop coming your way.

Ignore

Andrew tells you a joke and you ignore him. He starts to retell the joke, but you continue ignoring him. One more time he begins, and you continue to ignore Andrew and his attempt to bring humor to you. You not only give no response but you don't make eye contact. You have *disregarded* Andrew. Not only will you not hear any more of Andrew's jokes but your relationship with him may need to be repaired in other areas.

Positive reinforcement, negative reinforcement, punishment, and ignoring others produce consistent results. Which of these four ways do *you* use most often with your children, spouse, co-workers, and families? Or is there one you use more often with a particular person than another? Of the four ways, which way do you feel will lead to positively powerful results?

You can use these communication techniques with yourself too. When you do a great job and meet or exceed your expectations, give yourself some positive reinforcement! For me I reward myself after a speech with a luscious piece of chocolate candy, a good book, making a phone call to a friend I haven't spoken to in a while, or a little retail-therapy at my favorite mall.

Motivational speaker Carole Copeland Thomas offers these thoughts on positive self-talk in her book *Personal Empowerment:* "When was the last time you told yourself, 'I love you?' Have you complimented yourself on how gifted you are?....It's easy to slip into the habit of being particularly tough on yourself, zeroing in on that unwanted pimple or concentrating on the extra pounds that don't want to melt away....It takes extra effort to minimize our self-criticism by doubling the amount of time we use to celebrate what makes us so special."

To complete this chapter, please provide yourself with positive reinforcement by completing the follow sentences.

- What I appreciate most about myself is…

- One goal that I have accomplished that I would be proud to share is…

- The ways that I will reward myself for accomplishing future goals is…

- I will give myself positive reinforcement by (date)
  _____

Chapter Two

The Power of Feedback

Feedback is not good or bad, positive or negative, right or wrong. It is neutral information. And fortunately, it is always available.

As the last chapter showed, what we do and say makes an impact on others. We are always making a difference. The question we're going to tackle now is, "What kind?"

Have you ever asked yourself questions like these? "I wonder what I said or did that made them act like that?" "Why didn't I get the promotion I worked so hard for?" "How can I be a better mother/father?" "I did what I did last time; why didn't I get the same result?" These questions have to do with our impact, and we can only know this by checking with the person or people we made an impact on. Another way of saying this is we *need to get their feedback.*

If you want to be successful, remember *feedback is a gift*. It is information we can receive about our performance. It tells us how we are doing as we move towards our goal. As the diagram on page 5 showed, we each have our own beliefs systems. What you may believe may or may not be what the other person believes. And the only way you can find out is by asking them.

One of the beliefs that get in the way of our accepting feedback is that feedback is *criticism*. Criticism is about judging right or wrong. Feedback is neutral information, so there is no such thing as positive or negative, constructive or destructive, right or wrong, good or bad feedback. It just *is*. It's feedback in the same way that the speedometer in your car gives you feedback on the speed you are driving. Can you imagine going through a hospital zone at 65 miles an hour when the speed limit is 25 M.P.H. and thinking, "You're a bad speedometer for criticizing me." The speedometer is just doing its job, giving you information. It is up to you what you do with this knowledge.

If you want to be a positively powerful person you have to eliminate these other beliefs about feedback: Feedback can hurt someone's feelings. If you give feedback, say something good, and then give the feedback. Feedback isn't nice to give. *If any of these beliefs are yours, get rid of them.*

I was raised hearing, "If you can't say something good, don't say anything" so I was one of those who resisted hearing anything that I did not want to hear about my mediocre performance. If I was doing a good job, I wanted the praise, but the other kind of information? Not today.

Then I read a statement backed by research that turned this belief around for me. Here is what I read:

It's a sad fact but most people do not have access to the feedback they need to do a quality job. With effective feedback, improvements ranging from 20 to 600% aren't unusual.

Dr. Aubrey C. Daniels

When I read that, I decided that *anything* that could increase my results 600% was something I needed to make my friend and understand better. Don't we all want to be more successful?

Can you imagine bowling and not knowing how many pins you knocked down? Flying a plane without any instruments? Learning how to be a world class champion without a coach? Creating a business without a bank account? The score, instruments, coaches, and financial results are examples of *feedback.* How much more effective would you be if you knew beyond a shadow of a doubt how it was that you produced the results that you did? *Without feedback there is no learning.* If you know this, your chance of producing successful results increases dramatically

Everyone needs feedback! And it is a gift to *give* as well as to receive. Being able to give *others* feedback effectively is a skill that will lead to your success.

The following diagram takes the belief model and adds in the component of feedback so that you can see how it impacts your actions.

Feedback Contributes To Your Success

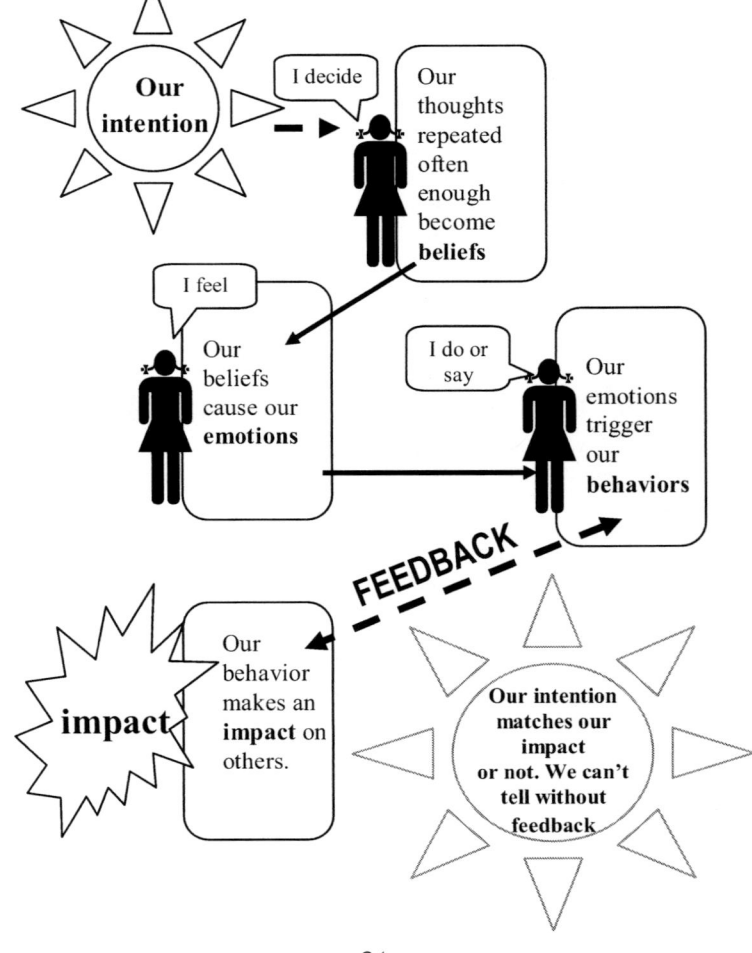

I have a good friend that used to frown and raise her voice when she got passionate about something. The message her frown sent to me was that she was angry. Coming from a family where conflict was to be avoided at all costs, I needed to consciously listen to her and adjust my feelings.

When I told her the message she was sending to me, she said, "Oh, I didn't know. Thank you." Being committed to making a positive impact, she changed her facial expression upon realizing that there may be other people who would react in the same way. And for those times when she still frowned and raised her voice with passion, I knew that we understood each other. You see, feedback is a powerful form of communication.

If your goal is to improve your relationships you will need *feedback*. Here are some tips to remember on giving and receiving feedback:

Receiving Feedback

- Feedback is always available. It is required to enhance your performance in anything. Remember, it can enhance your performance *600%!*

- If you need clarification, ask "what did I *say*" or "what did I *do*" so that you will receive behaviorally-based examples in return. This will allow you to amend, or alter, your actions appropriately.

- Remember that your feelings are your responsibility; they are triggered by your beliefs, and so your beliefs may not be the same as the person who is giving you the feedback.

- It is a gift. So say "thank you" when you get it.

Giving Feedback

- Before giving it, ask for permission from the other person.

- Be sincere. Feedback is not the time to get back at someone or to be self-righteous.

- When you give feedback on the behavior, do not target the person. Let your information be objective - factual, observable, measurable, etc. If you need to explain your feelings, be responsible for them. Remember they are *yours*.

- Use "I" statements.

- Speak directly to the other person and use eye contact if it is culturally acceptable. (In some cultures, eye contact is discourteous.)

- Give them information on what they did or said that worked, didn't work, or could work better if….

- Have a positive intention behind your words, and assume that they have a positive intention in listening to you.

> Feedback should describe problematic behavior that the receiver can correct. Ideally, it will be offered in response to the receiver's request, but whether or not it is solicited, effective feedback should be timely, clear, and accurate.
>
> Sue DeWine
> The Ohio University School of Interpersonal Communication

Knowledge without application is useless. You want to commit to making feedback a part of your life. So here are questions for you to consider about feedback.

1. What areas do you want to improve?

2. Who can you count on to give you feedback about how you come across or your performance in those areas?

3. Are you willing to ask this person to give you feedback, and will you *listen without being defensive*? If no, why not? If yes, when will you have this conversation with them?

4. You now are blessed to have a coach. What support will you give to them?

5. How can you support others through your feedback?

Chapter Three

The Power of Education

> Somewhere beyond the grief, fear, pain, and disappointment is a mighty lesson just waiting to be learned.
>
> Iyanla Vanzant
Yoruba Priestess and Author

Feedback is a skill and like any other skill you need to be successful, you can learn how to give it and receive it. Are there other skills you need to go where you want to go? If so, what must you learn? Is it a new belief? Or a new skill?

Here are a few learning goals that people have shared with me as they've progressed on their way to dream fulfillment:

- How to manage a workforce effectively.

- How to be a better time manager.

- How to be better at speaking in front of large groups.
- How to empower others as a leader.
- How to increase personal or business finances.
- How to be vulnerable.
- How to be a committed listener.
- How to write a book.
- How to be more assertive.
- How to increase self-esteem.
- How to become an entrepreneur.
- How to resolve conflicts.
- How to experience fulfillment and peace.

It's a fact: You can learn anything that you want.
A way to start the process of pursuing and achieving knowledge or learning a new skill is to make a contract with yourself such as the one that follows. To complete yours, fill in the rest of each statement.

Learning Contract

1. I would like to learn…

   _____

   _____

   _____

2. The benefits to me in learning this are…

   _____

   _____

   _____

3. My life will be better when I reach my learning goal because…

   _____

   _____

   _____

4. Achieving my learning goal will make others' lives better because…

   _____

   _____

   _____

5. I need these resources (people, places, networks, money, time, libraries, websites, etc.) to achieve my learning goal:

_____

_____

_____

6. The challenges that may lie before me that I will conquer in order to learn are…

_____

_____

7. I will overcome them by being the following ways (characteristics) and doing the following things:

_____

_____

_____

_____

8. I will accomplish my goal by (cite a date)

_____

*Signed By*_____ *Today's Date*_____

Congratulations!

Being Aware

The Brahman Dona saw the Buddha sitting under a tree and was impressed by his peaceful air of alertness and his good looks.

He asked the Buddha:
"Are you a god?"
"No, Brahman, I am not a god."

"Then an angel?"
"No, indeed, Brahman."

"A spirit, then?"
"No, I am not a spirit."
"Then what are you?"
"I am awake."

Anguttara Nikaya
From "Buddha Speaks," edited by
Anne Bancroft

I can learn anything I want!

I am my own best teacher.
And I am a very good student.
I can be taught by me
whatever I put my heart, soul, and mind to.

I am never too old to learn.
I patiently handle all challenges of learning.
It is up to no one else but me to be brilliant,
to be courageous
in my mental development,
to be self-correcting,
and to be outrageous in my educational goals.

Every day
I am more and more aware of myself.
Every day
the subjects of my choosing become clearer.
Every day
I am a miraculous learner.
Every day
I can learn anything I want.

Joel Martin

Whatever you want to learn you can learn. There is a Senegalese Proverb that says, "The opportunity that God sends does not wake up him who is asleep." So have *faith.*

Faith is the certainty that you will prevail even when there is no rational evidence. Faith is knowing that step by step you will get to your mountaintop. Faith is believing in a higher power that will assist you on your way. *If you can dream it, you can achieve it--believe it!*

Positively powerful people
are lifelong learners.

I myself woke up to my love of learning late in life. At the time I had become curious about what it was about experiential trainings that made them so effective. For example, why was the simulation of a near-death experience so effective that people left the training eager to let their loved ones know how much they cared about them and hungry to discover what living passionately was all about for them?

I wondered, how did this training work begin? Who had started it and why? When I went back to school to find out, I thought that I would feel out of place. I was about 50 miles outside my comfort zone!

I didn't even know if I'd be successful and able to keep up. But to my surprise, I discovered that I loved learning! I wasn't out of place at all. In fact, I contributed to the other students through exhibiting my maturity, expressing my life experiences, and revealing my commitment to learning.

Only by stepping out and risking did I create the spectacular results. I grew, and as I did, I continued to learn about myself and others. I moved from being "an eight-year-old liar" to having a Masters and a Ph.D., and being a Wharton Business School Fellow. *If I can do it, you can too!*

Teach It to Keep It

Research says we retain 5% of the information we hear from lectures or from someone talking to us; 10% of what we read; 20% from audio-visual means (films, slides, PowerPoint presentations, music); 30% from what is shown to us; and 50% from a group discussion. However, we retain 75% from practicing, experiencing, having on-the-job training, and doing; and 80% when we are teaching and using.

So teach what you learn to others. *It will stay with you longer.*

Chapter Four

The Power of Make-Believe

The mind commands the body and it obeys. The mind orders itself and meets resistance.

St. Augustine
Born in Souk Ahras, Algeria, North Africa

When I was a little girl, I read a lot and found reading a great escape. My four favorite words were "Once upon a time" because I knew that what followed would take me to the land of make-believe with fascinating people, places, and activities. In those pages of fantasy I learned that I could dream about how I wished things could be.

Books became the places to lose myself. The Little Golden Book series and the single title The *Little Engine That Could*, for example, gave my mother's words, "You can be anything you want, even the president" positive reinforcement. I learned to use my imagination to take me through the scary places of my childhood.

The ability to dream begins within us. As adults we tend to diminish this quality and encourage our little ones to pay attention to the 'real world' rather than the world of the imagination. Perhaps you are one of those who were told to "stop daydreaming." The ability to dream, to imagine a reality through internal visualization, is a strength to be treated with respect. It is "the ability to confront and deal with reality by using the creative power of the mind (GuruNet)."

Think about the word "make." It means to cause to exist or happen, to bring about, to manifest. And the word "believe" is the mental process whereby we hold an interpretation to be a reality and act accordingly. So when we *make-believe* we are bringing forth a reality using our imagination, our minds, and our hearts.

Keep thy heart (or imagination) with all diligence, for out of it are the issues of life.

Prov. 4:23

Your brain is a wonderful creation. Through your senses, your brain captures sound waves. This is true whether you send the message, or someone else does. *If you want to enhance your personal power, however, be mindful of the messages you speak about yourself and about others.* If you want to create something, speak in the *positive about what you are committed to,* and not in the negative about what you are not committed to. In my trainings I say, "Do not think of a purple elephant…with a green monkey on its back wearing a blue hat. No matter what, do not think of the elephant."

What does the mind "see"? The purple elephant with the green monkey in all of its blue-hatted splendor. Similarly, if you are nervous about an upcoming event, the most powerful way to speak about it to yourself and others is through using the words "I am courageous" rather than "I will not be afraid." The latter expression presences "afraid" in the mind, just like a purple elephant.

To get yourself in the mindset of creative imagery, relax, breathing deeply and slowly several times in a row. Clear your mind and allow yourself some quiet time alone. Humbly ask the Divine to assist you and guide you on your way. Recognize that it is the will of the Divine that what you dream to create will be yours in healthy, happy, peaceful, joyous, abundant, and prosperous ways. During this time allow for harmony in the body, mind, and spirit.

Now that you've prepared your mind to accept your dream, there are at least four ways that you can further your positive power using the skill of *make-believe*. The four ways are: affirmations, standing in the future, positive imagery, and reframing.

Affirmation

An *affirmation* is when you, with authority, declare for something that you do not possess but are passionately committed to having. You speak the affirmation aloud, using positive words and the present tense. To anchor your affirmation, write it on a 3X5 card and post it by your mirror. Repeat it during the day and especially before you go to sleep at night. I have my affirmations on my computer screen saver and update them according to my manifestation of them.

Here are some examples of affirmations:

- I love everyone and everyone loves me.

- I speak in ways that empower my co-workers and receive abundant sums of money as a result.

- I am an excellent listener.

- I have more than enough time to spend with my wife, children, and friends.

From *Wisdom of Florence Scovel Shinn*:

- Large sums of money come to me quickly in divine ways. I have more than enough for my personal and professional needs.

- I am now on the royal road of Success, Happiness and Abundance, all traffic goes my way.

Standing in the Future

Make-believe that you have a dream for a new career. Imagine what that career would be, what would you be doing in this career, what would you be saying on the job, what kinds of people you would be working with, how much money you would be making, and so forth.

Now imagine that your dream *has already come true*. In fact, we meet while you have been in your new career for six months and you, with a lot of excitement, are telling me about it. You tell me *the story* about it as though it – the future – were occurring right now.

How would you be describing your new career? You probably would be saying something like, "Today was a great day, and I was busy today in my new career. I really like the people that I work with. They are brilliant! My new career is very fulfilling, and I'm well-paid for what I do."

Today, in real time, you may be unhappy in your actual job, or bored, or underemployed, or wanting to start your own company. However, the technique of *standing in the future* allows you to imagine out loud the different scenarios, challenges, opportunities, resources, and accomplishments associated with your goal or vision. To pretend that it is so in the present. *There are no negatives associated with this process.* Your brain gets the message and triggers emotions that you experience as though the future has actually occurred!

I encourage you to test this technique and experience the positive power you can tap into with this method. Here's how:

- *Bring to mind your vision/goal/new career – whatever your dream is.* Write a few paragraphs. Include who, what, when, where, how, and why to the best of your ability. The "why" part is very important because it takes into account the significance of the dream to you.

Example: My goal is to build a dream home in Arizona some day. I love the area and I am ready to give up shoveling snow. In addition, the area is one of the quickest growing in the U.S. I have my own business and I am sure that there would be many new opportunities for me if I lived there. Also, I want to live in a beautiful environment.

- *Share your story* with a friend over lunch or some other time when you can spend at least one hour together. Let your friend know that you will be sharing a story about your future and that you will be telling the story about the future dream or goal *in the present tense*, as though it were occurring right now. "I will" and "I want to" becomes "I am." "Someday" becomes the present.

  Example: I have moved into my beautiful home. It is a one-story stucco with three bedrooms and a sunken living room in the Arizona mountains. The air is warm, the cacti have started blooming, and I am standing by my pool. I have just finished a coaching call with one of my new corporate clients. The call went very well and the client has referred me to others. I am building a very profitable business, meeting many new friends, and in my spare time am volunteering in a community organization. I am so glad that I moved!

- Let your friend know that this is something that is important to you and their input is appreciated. Their role is to assist you in telling the story. Coach your friend to ask you for more details. *Invite him or her to challenge you* with spontaneous daring questions about your new 'reality.'

Examples of questions your friend might ask: *Who* are you with? *What* did you say that caused you to get the coaching contract? *When* exactly did it occur? *How* did you accomplish that? *Why* a one story home? *Where* is the guest room? *What* was important to you? *What* obstacles did you face? *How* did you overcome the obstacles? I am coming to visit; do you have a fire place?

- Your friend can also assist you by making sure you use the *standing in the future* guidelines:
  a. Tell the story about your new career or other dream.
  b. Speak in the present tense. ("I am" rather than "I will".)
  c. Speak freely and spontaneously. Resist the temptation to edit yourself.
  d. Include the ways you overcame obstacles, who you enrolled onto your team, the strategies you used, and the difference you made with others.

- e. Respond and answer the questions your friend asks of you.
- f. Have fun.

- After sharing your story, notice what you have been feeling. What emotions were triggered through this process for you? Usually people are excited, enthusiastic, empowered, hopeful, and see the future more clearly.

- Notice how your friend responds to what you are saying and feeling as you talk about your desired future using present tense verbs. Most listeners are excited and happy for you. They will want you to let them know how you do in the future. *They are now on your team.*

- If you like, ask your friend if he or she would like to *stand in the future* with his or her own goals. If "yes," be ready to respond with a good measure of your time, enthusiasm, questions, and willingness to assist your friend in *following the guidelines*.

Now that you have talked about your "current reality" in the positive, what message do you think you are sending to your brain? How do you think it would be different if you talked about such a future negatively?

Corporations do a version of this called *scenario planning*.

> Scenarios are specially constructed stories about the future. Each scenario represents a distinct, plausible world. The purpose of scenario planning is not to predict the future; but rather, to show how different forces can manipulate the future in different directions. When this is accomplished, the ability to better respond to future events is increased.
>
> Dr. Richard Smith
> edie.cprost.sfu.ca/~idea/scenarios.html

Positive Imagery

The next method of make-believe is *positive imagery*. With positive imagery you use your imagination to see a positive and complete picture of yourself *after* you have accomplished your desired outcome. It is a process that you do alone.

Athletes know and use positive imagery to improve their abilities and outcome. Those seeking to lose weight use it to keep their mind on their goal. When I am about to deliver a speech or training, I imagine myself at the successful conclusion of the event.

It might also help to make a *concrete representation* of what you imagine for the future. This is another kind of positive imagery. For example, you can create a collage of photographs from magazines that portray what it is that you want to create or do. Then hang the collage where you can view it easily every day; this will inspire you to work towards your goal.

Reframing

With the last make-believe technique, reframing, you speak about an event or situation *with the intention of changing how you feel about the event.* I find this method especially useful in empowering myself to change my story from a negative one to a positive one. For example, I could have gone through life telling the "dumb 8-year old liar" story as though I were the ultimate victim. *Poor me.* But this would lead to my feeling unworthy, pitiful, and incapable...a negatively disempowered person. Yuck! So, instead, I chose to reframe it as an example to learn from of how I let my beliefs impact my life. In addition, if I hadn't focused on my artistic talent as a result of avoiding writing in the future, I never would have been creative director of an ad agency. This event was *good news*. So in this way, the event is a *gift* to me. Reframed, my story becomes a bridge that I can use to reach others and many find that they relate to it.

I once heard someone ask, "If your friends talked to you the way *you* talk to you, would you still consider them your friends?" So as you consider your own success and how you view your life, how do *you* talk to *you*? What are the words you use to describe yourself? What is your internal conversation about your potential, your dreams, and your possibilities?

We all have a "little voice" inside that gives us a running dialogue on everything about ourselves and around us. Do you support yourself most often with empowering sound bites like, "Yes, I can" or disempowering ones like "I'll never be able to do it" or "I'm not enough"?

Being responsible and powerful in any situation demands your ability to retell any story of what happened in a way that empowers you. You will learn to be accountable for your actions. This will lead to your *learning* from misfortune rather than being a *victim* of misfortune.

A broken relationship is just one event in your life. Don't make it your whole story.

Dr. Gwendolyn Grant
Author and Columnist

As with the other *make-believe* technologies, in *reframing* you use your words and imagination to trigger new experiences and forwarding feelings, to empower others, and to walk the talk as a positively powerful person. In reframing we hang the picture in a different frame so that everyone gets a different look.

Let's take stock of where you are now. Write down in as much detail as you can your response to the following:

- *Practice standing in the future:* What is your goal? Your dream? Your vision? Write as though the pinnacle of success was reached last year and you are writing to a friend with whom you haven't talked in a long time. You are telling them about what you created last year. Next, go out and have that fun lunch with the friend whom you will tell about your vision as though it were happening in real-time.

- What *affirmation* have you selected to inspire you? There are many books that include affirmations, such as *Feel the Fear and Do It Anyway* by Susan Jeffers, Ph.D., *Acts of Faith* by Iyanla Vanzant, or *In the Spirit,* by Susan Taylor. If you haven't found affirmations that you like or that define your needs, create one for yourself. Remember: *Present tense and positive words only.* Then say your affirmation every day. So be it!

- *Reframing*: What areas of your life do you need to reframe? What conversations about your past do you need to reframe?

- Lastly, have you included *positive imagery* in your daily routines?

Chapter Five

The Power of Choice

Ayu dame a tomar responsibilidad por mi propia vida para que, por fin, pueda ser libre.

Help me take responsibility for my own life so that I can be free at last.

Cesar Estrada Chavez
Founder, The United Farm Workers (UFW)

To demonstrate how the power of *make-believe* can shape your feelings, behaviors, and, by extension, your outcomes, here is a simulation that dates from early interpersonal experiential education. It has given many people access to their power source.

Simulation

Make a list of the things that you *have to do*. In this case, *have to* means you don't like doing them most of the time, you feel forced to do them, and that you feel you have *no choice* about doing them. You do them only because of duty and obligation.

For example, "I *have to* cook dinner even though I'm tired." "I *have to* pay bills and I don't like to, but I pay them any way." "I *have to* answer emails and do performance reviews on my employees" and so on.

Make sure that you write "I *have to*" before each item if you are using a separate piece of paper. And say each phrase out loud as you write the words. Writing and saying those three words, "*I have to*", is a very important part of the experiment.

I have to_____

I have to_____

I have to_____

I have to_____

I have to_____

I have to_____

In addition to the things we *have to* do, there are the ways we *have to* be. For example, "I *have to* be polite to customers at all times no matter what." "I *have to be* nice to all of my relatives." "I *have to* be a strong person."

Add to your existing list all the ways you can think of that you *have to* be. And again, say each phrase out loud.

I have to be_____

I have to be_____

I have to be_____

I have to be_____

I have to be_____

I have to be_____

After you've written out the list, take another minute or so to read what you've written. If there is anything that you've left off, include it at this time. Give yourself at least five minutes to think about what you may have left off.

Next, write down the *feelings* you have as a result of expressing your *have to do's* and *be's*: As a result of thinking and writing about what I say I *have to do* and *be*, I feel:

_____

_____

_____

_____

_____

The emotions that I hear expressed in relation to the *have to's* are usually sadness, depression, frustration, anger, numbness, a sense of being trapped, and so on. What were yours?

Now, take three deep breaths of air to clear out the *have to's*. You are about to shift gears.

It's time to write and say out loud yet another list, this time of the things you choose to do and be. Examples can include, "I *choose to* cook." "I *choose to* play with my children." "I *choose to* be polite to our customers." "I *choose to* pay my bills." And so on.

I choose to_____

I choose to_____

I choose to_____

I choose to_____

I choose to_____

I choose to_____

In addition to the things we *choose to* do, there are the ways we *choose to* be. Add to your list ways you *choose to* be.

I choose to be_____

I choose to be_____

I choose to be_____

I choose to be_____

I choose to be_____

I choose to be_____

Now write down the feelings that came up for you in writing the *choose to* list: As a result of thinking and writing about what I say I *choose to do* and *be*, I feel…

_____

_____

_____

_____

Next deliberately include some of the *have to's* from your first list as items on your new *choose to* list. Notice what, if anything, changes in how you feel about the activities you do or attributes you be. No matter what the activity or attribute is, write and say out loud "I do not *have to*, I *choose to*" before it. Here's the format:

I do not *have to*, I *choose to* _____

_____

I do not *have to*, I *choose to* _____

_____

I do not *have to*, I *choose to* _____

_____

I do not *have to*, I *choose to* _____

_____

I do not *have to*, I *choose to* _____

_____

I do not *have to*, I *choose to* _____

_____

Now write down the feelings that came up for you in writing and speaking the new phrases of the simulation: As a result of changing the words I use from I *have to do/be* to I *choose to do/be*, I feel...

_____

_____

_____

_____

_____

Did your feelings change from what you expressed in regards to your first *have to do/be* list? They usually do.

The emotions that I usually hear expressed about the *choose to's* are a sense of freedom, happiness, relief, relaxation, peacefulness, joy, and more. Did your list reflect such a change?

What did you learn from this *have to -- choose to* simulation? Which words contribute more to your feeling like a positively powerful person? Which words lead to your having the most positive effect on others?

Here is space to write what you learned and want to remember through the simulation:

_____

_____

_____

_____

_____

_____

_____

_____

_____

In your choice of language there is power. That's because *you* decide the words you use!

The difference between a *have to* and a *choose to* is all about *attitude* and *perception*. So decide what words you will use and what attitude is important based on what matters to you and is the highest and best use of you.

But I must caution you: You may *choose to* get attention, have a pity party, get angry, blame others, not be responsible, or act worthless. That is your right. However, the prices are high because in time, the conscious and disempowering choices you have made will become unconscious and automatic. You will have effectively sabotaged your ability to be a positively powerful person. You will become known as an angry person, a blaming person, an irresponsible person, a sad person… not a *bad* person, just not a powerful one.

The most powerful way to act is *as if you chose everything, including your attitude.* Notice I did not say that you do, *in fact,* chose everything. Rather I said *to act* as though you do.

This brings us to responsibility. This word has many connotations. When we break the word into its two parts it is literally the ability to respond. Some people think of responsibility as a duty or obligation. When they use this definition, responsibility often comes across like a *have to*. Another definition for responsibility implies legal, financial, or moral accountability. And yet another is that of existentialist, Jean-Paul Satre who wrote that to be responsible is to be the "uncontested author of an event or a thing." This latter definition is the one that I use in my work.

When you take this stand of responsibility, you are saying that you have the power to choose and are accountable for the choices you make. This is a critical distinction in the transformational work that I do.

It is as though when you were born you were given a ticket that said…

> **WELCOME TO LIFE, LITTLE ONE.**
> **THIS IS YOUR TICKET.**
> **ADMIT ONE.**
> *From this point on everything is your choice.*

Living life this way means that you own your attitudes, choices, actions, results, breakdowns, breakthroughs, values, suffering, joy, beliefs, and all other aspects of who you are and what you do. You own your faith and your Divinity as well.

Being responsible means that you *get to* and *chose to* give up being a victim of anything, of anyone, and of any circumstances. *You can do something about anything because you are in ownership of it.* You are free to create all of the wondrous ideas of your dreams. You are the source. *If it's to be, it's up to thee.*

Don't get me wrong: you may give up being a victim, but there still will be bad things that happen to good, responsible people. So it is important to understand the difference between *being a victim* and *being victimized*. Being a victim is living a life of powerlessness and blaming others. These people make personal and professional decisions in the "now" based on baggage from their past. This is not bad or wrong, but *living life this way will not lead to fulfillment.*

Being victimized means something else. There are whole races of people who have been victimized systematically because of the color of their skin, the slant of their eyes, their sexual orientation, their gender, their language, their religion, and/or the natural resources of their country. Racist victimization is intolerable. Yet in this miasma of "isms" and despair, shining examples of men and women who refused to let their victimization determine who they are exist to empower us all.

There are notable role models like publisher of *Black Enterprise* magazine Earl G. Graves, the first Black president of South Africa Nelson Mandela, civil rights activist Susan B. Anthony, founder of the National Council of Negro Women Dr. Dorothy Height, and so many others that I could mention. There are also hundreds of thousands of every-day heroes whose names wouldn't be recognizable but who also prove that people can be victimized and not be victims.

Here is an opportunity for you to take a look at the choices you make regarding your attitude. There are three possibilities. These scenarios are about the attitude you choose for the event called work. (Please note: "Work" can include wherever you spend most of your time each day, whether it's working at a 9-to-5 job, being mom or dad to three children each day, or being a world class athlete. Just adapt the scenarios that follow to fit your unique work situation.)

Scenario One
You typically greet co-workers and your boss with a "Glad to be here. Let's have something great happen today" attitude and a smile. You act as someone who's about the business of creating success in his or her world. You notice people ask for your opinion a lot. You leave any negative baggage in the past and are totally present in the moment. You are a team player.

Scenario Two
You go to work with an "I don't want to be here. I don't like being here. I *have to* be here" attitude. You come across as negative, resistant, and angry, even if it's passively angry. You bear grudges. You notice that people move out of your way a lot. You may do a good job but it may only be enough to get by and not your best effort. You find yourself blaming others for situations that arise.

Scenario Three

You come across with an "I don't care" attitude of someone who's already RIPed -- retired in place. You are always the last one to arrive at meetings, and no one seems to even notice. You feel tired and bored.

These scenarios may seem like a bit of an exaggeration, but regardless, *take stock of your attitude. How do you show up at work?*
- Positively Powerful (Scenario #1)
- Rigidly Resistant (Scenario #2)
- Complacently RIPped, Retired In Place (Scenario #3)

How are you with your family and friends? Your community? It all boils down to whether you are you *giving* or *taking*. Positively powerful people are contributors. They give, and give again. Rigidly resistant and complacently RIPpeds are not...they take, sit there, and take again.

Perhaps you may be thinking, "Well, other people *make me* have that attitude." If so, know that *make me* is just a different way of saying *have to*. Either way you are still *choosing* how you want to be.

The same event can occur, but a different decision and hence a different attitude choice made by you can ensure *a different outcome*. If you were the boss in your organization, whom would you *choose* to promote? The positively powerful person or the rigidly resistant? Whom would you give the raise to? Whom would you give a great recommendation to?

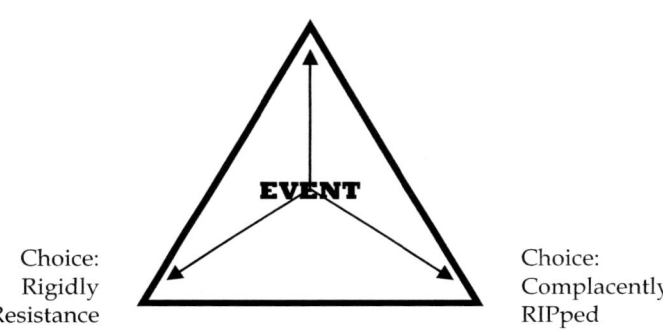

If you are the boss of your own company, what's the message you are sending your customers, your suppliers, or your employees? That you're angry, ornery, pissed-off, unlikable, and resistant in your dealings with them? Dried-up, uncaring, complacent, tired, bored, and RIPped? Or are you and your company employees visionary, creative, current, and resourceful – in other words, positively powerful?

Positively powerful people choose their attitude based on their vision.

Your ability to choose your attitude is the difference - figuratively and literally - between your success and just getting by, between life and death. In the book *Man's Search for Meaning*, Viktor Frankl, the Austrian psychiatrist imprisoned in the death camps of Nazi Germany in World War II, tells how he exercised his power to choose his response to the terrible conditions to which he was subjected (the Nazis conducted experiments on his body). He discovered, "I have the power to choose". He believed that if you have a meaning (purpose or cause), if you have a *why*, you can live with any *what*.

Nelson Mandela was the president of South African from 1994 to 1999. He was imprisoned for nearly 30 years for his anti-apartheid activities. Released in 1990, he led the African National Congress in negotiating an end to apartheid. In 1993 he shared the Nobel Peace Prize. Even though he spent 30 years of his life imprisoned, he was not a prisoner. He was a *free* man while in prison. As with Viktor Frankl, Mandela's circumstances did not determine his reality. His *why*, his mission, empowered him to handle any *what*.

Another of my heroes is Dr. Maya Angelou. As a child she was mute for nearly five years because of a brutal act of violence. (Read her book *I Know Why The Caged Bird Sings*.) Today Dr. Angelou speaks numerous languages fluently, was the recipient of the Yale University Fellowship, and was the poet laureate for a U.S. President. To me, her life story is a testimony to what is possible when we choose from our purpose, vision, and mission. Her *why* and her courage allowed her withstand any *what*.

The impact of choice also shows up in business results. A study done by Texas Instruments showed that the best predictor of a project's failure or success was whether people volunteered or had been told they had been assigned to the project. With the implied choice of volunteering came *100% ownership* of the quality of the communications, relationships, and the project's results. These employees did things they probably would not have undertaken in a mandatory situation.

This experiment implies that if we want to empower others it's best if we consciously honor their ability to choose and provide them with options. We can't control anyone but we can empower them to take actions that lead to wins.

Having the power to choose does not mean that we control the situation. Control is an illusion.

We have no control over anything any more than we can control the sun, moon, stars, or heavens. What we seek when we say *control* is that we want a certainty, a guarantee, and dominance. No matter how much we might want something we just might not get it. Or we might. *There's no guarantee.*

The trick is in *acting* as though you absolutely will, and having a "Yes, I can" winning attitude as you move towards your goals. In other words, life is a journey, not a destination.

> There is no path to happiness and peace.
> Happiness and peace is the way.
>
> A Buddhist Expression

Here is an example of a personal dilemma related to control that I've experienced and one to which you might relate: My husband Bob and I are the parents of a beautiful daughter who is a cinematographer. Her goal is to shoot multi-million dollar features. I saw her once high up in the air on a crane with a camera doing her magic: she was part mathematician, part painter, part lighting alchemist, and all professional. My husband and I are very proud of her.

Yet my pride is edged with frustration that has to do with my inability to *control*. When Cybel was a child, her comfort, well-being, and joy were more easily within my grasp.

Now that she is an adult, it is frustrating that I cannot make the world give her her dreams. I can support her, but I can't control the results of her actions. So I do all that I can and then I do my best to surrender to the trust that one day she will walk on the red carpet at the NAACP, Sundance, Oscars, and other award ceremonies as an internationally renowned director of photography. I have faith, and simply *choose to* believe that she will be awarded for her performance.

What I am learning from this is that by relinquishing my need to control events and people's actions, *I have less stress and worry.* I am more appreciative of the times we have as a family, and Cybel and I have a lot more fun together. So, to all who seek to control, whether it be for your child, career, goals or world, just *surrender*. At the point when you have done all you can, *let go and let God* take over. Have faith.

Here is a poem for those of you who have experienced a similar emotion regarding your children.

On Children

And a woman who held a babe against
her bosom said, Speak to us of Children.
And he said: Your children are not your children.
They are the sons and daughters of Life's longing
for itself. They come through you but not from
you. And though they are with you yet they
belong not to you.
You may give them your love but not your
thoughts, for they have their own thoughts.
You may house their bodies but not their souls. For
their souls dwell in the house of tomorrow, which
you cannot visit, not even in your dreams.
You may strive to be like them, but seek not to
make them like you. For life goes not backward
nor tarries with yesterday.

Kahil Gibran, *The Prophet*
Author, poet, philosopher, and artist. Born in Lebanon.

Chapter Six

The Power of Responsibility and Accountability

I've had enough of someone else's propaganda. I'm for truth, no matter who tells it. I'm for justice, no matter who it is for or against. I'm a human being first and foremost, and as such, I'm for whoever and whatever benefits humanity as a whole.

EL-Hajj Malik Shabaz · Malcolm X

Living responsibly and accountably are attributes of the positively powerful person.

- Responsibly: "I have the ability to choose. I am the source."

- Accountably: "I have the ability to account for the specific choices I made that led to this event. I am relating."

With accountability, you are using your ability to go back in time and explain the chain of events that led to a particular outcome. You provide a narrative and recall the events as a responsible person who made the decisions.

Here is a version of a true experience that reveals the power of accountability. I had a friend who asked me to be a consultant to him on a contract he had with a national nonprofit organization. Knowing about my ad agency experience, he asked me to design and have printed a souvenir journal for the organization. I received an advance, or a prepayment of a portion of the total estimated fee, from him. I then proceeded to create a product that made both my friend and the client very happy. Yet my friend never finished paying for my time even though it ended up being a rush job that required additional overtime charges. My friend had signed a contract with me and had received my invoices, yet he never sent the balance of the payment.

It would be easy to say that I was victimized by him. However, I can account for the decisions I made that led to the outcome. The first one was I accepted the job. The next was that I signed a contract *with my friend* and not the client who was paying for the job. The third was that even though he missed sending a payment partway through the process, I continued working with him. Why? Because I had given my word to complete the job. Each step along the way *I* made a decision. I was in the driver's seat. It was easy being accountable when things went the way I wanted them to, but it was harder when they did not, and it has taken me some time to get to the

Chapter Ten

The Power of Dedication

You can be anything you want to be, even the president!

Ann Kenney McLaurin
Mother, sister, friend, and neighbor

Imagine that your goals, meaningful existence, most heartfelt desire, the way you want to live, your business success, the relationship you desire, and your dreams are represented by objects sitting safely on top of a snow-covered mountain.

There is a safe path up to the spot and you take it. Along the way there would be a blizzard, extreme cold, strong winds, and low visibility. It's a "whiteout" on the mountain. Intuitively you know that your "it" is up there (The "it" is your vision.), but since you can't see where you're going, the path to your achievement is going to be invisible and unknown. So you don't know with certainty that you will achieve your vision.

Nevertheless, you move forward. All the while you ask, "Is this going to work? Did I take all the proper steps, ask all the right questions, and network with enough people, the right people...?" And along your path you revel in the outbursts of joy, the excitement, and the empowerment you have shared with others of what your success would look like, feel like, and be like when you have achieved it. This is what keeps you going forward on the path. *You are dedicated, and you are a positively powerful person.*

With you, you have the powerful forces you have generated and you intend to use them!

The power of beliefs

The power of feedback to check where you are

The power of education

The power of make-believe

The power of choice

The power of responsibility and accountability

The power of values

The power of purpose

The power of vision and the 10 creation steps

The power of dedication

You are clear on your vision of success, and your core values are like "snow poles" -- stakes in the ground on the edge of the path that guide you up to the top. Your creation process is thorough, and your action plan has moved you up to the summit.

As you reach the summit you realize that there is another mountain peak in the distance. Your response to seeing that is, "Great...what's next for me that's up on that peak?!"

As you prepare to leave this summit and your current successes, you go down into another valley in order to climb to the next success, the next mountaintop.

You are light for the whole world. A city built on a hill cannot be hid. No one lights a lamp and puts it under a bowl; instead he puts it on the lamp stand where it gives light for everyone in the house. In the same way your light must shine before people so that they will see the good things you do and praise your Father in heaven.

Jesus Christ
Speaking to his Disciples in His Sermon on the Mount.
Matt. 5: 13-16

You are a Divinely-created, positively powerful person. The next mountaintop awaits you. You best be on your way.

My Impossible Thing

It may make me afraid. But it is possible.
It may seem out of reach. But it is possible.
It may demand my best. But it is possible.
It may challenge me, run from me, confront me. But it is possible
It may force me to face my doubt, turn me inside out. But it is possible
It may be tough. But it is possible.

I am the mistress of my fate,
the author of my story.
I can change the impossible into a possibility
and the possibility into a reality.
Through courage. With faith,
the impossible is possible.

Joel Martin

About The Author

Joel Martin, Ph.D. is an international trainer, behavioral scientist, public speaker, award-winning communicator, and entrepreneur. Born in New York City, Ms. Martin was to become one of first women to own and operate a full service advertising agency. She and her husband ran J. P. Martin Associates and assisted others in making their own history.

Ms. Martin learned many management *do's and don'ts* from these experiences and incorporated these lessons with her love of individual and organizational transformation to create Triad West, Inc.

Triad West, Inc. is a consulting, training, and motivational communications company headquartered in Scottsdale, Arizona. Its corporate mission is to contribute in measurable, sustainable and performance-related ways through products and services that embody excellence, responsibility, respect for diversity, and integrity.

Ms. Martin is a Wharton Fellow and earned a Masters in Psychology and a Ph.D. in Communications. She was a recipient of the Distinguished Alumni Award from Ohio State University and a delegate to the White House Conference on Small Business.

Her recognition includes Outstanding Young Women of America, Who's Who in the East, and International Who's Who of Entrepreneurs. She has been featured on the Today Show, and in the *New York Times*, *U.S. News and World Report*, *Essence*, *Black Enterprise*, *Fortune*, and *Working Women*.

Appreciation of her expertise has taken her across the United States, Puerto Rico, the Republic of South Africa, the United Kingdom, Latvia, Finland, Malaysia, and Russia.

Ms. Martin continues to be challenged and inspired by the thought, "Imagine how the world would be if *everyone* lived his or her dream."

We welcome your feedback, comments, suggestions, and requests for other motivational products. We would also like to know how *How To Be A Positively Powerful Person* impacted your life. To let us know, please visit www.triadwest.com.

If you would like to contact Triad West, Inc. for information about consulting and training services and/or are interested in having Joel Martin, Ph.D. speak at your event, please visit www.triadwest.com.

May all of your dreams for success come true!